America's Wetlands

Guide to Plants and Animals

Marianne D. Wallace

Fulcrum Publishing
Golden, Colorado

D0719940

Mallard

Pickerelweed

Leopard frog

Frog eggs

Spatterdock

I dedicate this book to the little treefrog that I found in the marshes near my home when I was 10 years old.* He (she?) helped teach me that nature is full of wondrous things.

Plants and animals shown on the front cover (clockwise from upper right): **Canada goose, moose, iris, great egret, pitcher plant growing out of sphagnum moss, slider (turtle), pied-billed grebe, alligator, duckweed, golden club, bald cypress, green darner (dragonfly), Spanish moss (hanging on bald cypress branches).**

Plants and animals shown on the back cover: (clockwise from upper right): **White pelican, branch of bald cypress, tule (hardstem bulrush), red-winged blackbird, leopard frog, swamp rose-mallow, mallard, ribbon snake, cattail, river otter, tiger swallowtail.**

Fulcrum Publishing

16100 Table Mountain Parkway, Suite 300

Golden, Colorado 80403

(800) 992-2908 • (303) 277-1623

www.fulcrum-books.com

*P.S. I kept the little guy (or gal, who knows) in a jar with twigs and rocks on my bathroom sink. Alas, the story does not have a happy ending: the rocks shifted—don't know how—and squished the little treefrog. But, I learned how to closely observe animals from the experience. That, and to stop and consider before taking any animal or plant out of its native habitat.

Text and illustrations copyright © 2004 Marianne D. Wallace

All rights reserved. No part of this book may be reproduced, stored in a retrieval system, or transmitted in any form or by any means, electronic, mechanical, photocopying, recording, or otherwise, without written permission from the publisher.

Library of Congress Cataloging-in-Publication Data
   Wallace, Marianne D.
     America's wetlands : guide to plants and animals / Marianne D. Wallace.
        p. cm.
     Includes index.
     ISBN 1-55591-484-5 (pbk. : alk. paper)
     1. Wetland animals--United States--Juvenile literature. 2. Wetland plants--United States--Juvenile literature. 3. Wetlands--United States--Juvenile literature. I. Title.
     QL155.W35 2004
     577.68'097--dc22

                              2004012365

ISBN 1-55591-484-5

Printed in China

0 9 8 7 6 5 4 3 2 1

Editorial: Katie Raymond
Design: Ann W. Douden
Cover image: Marianne D. Wallace

Marsh fern

Table of Contents

Mallard with ducklings

Pickerelweed

Tadpoles

Spatterdock   Leopard frog

Introduction to Wetlands Life

What do you think of when you imagine a wetland? Do you picture a marshy lake? A river? A swamp? Even if you're not sure what the word *wetland* means, you can probably figure out what all wetlands have in common: water.

The water in wetlands may come from rain, melted snow and ice, overflowing lakes and rivers, or water that has soaked into the ground and filled nearby low spots or depressions. The common names of some of the plants and animals that live in wetlands are clues to the types of wetlands you may find: **bog** rosemary, **marsh marigold**, **swamp rabbit**, and **river** otter. Other types of wetlands include fens, vernal pools, playas and other shallow lakes, potholes, muskegs, streambanks, flood plains, creeks, and sloughs. Even edges of ponds and lakes can become wetland homes for plants and animals. Almost any area that is wet for at least part of every year can be a wetland.

Swamp rabbit and marsh marigold

Map of Earth.
Wetlands cover about $\frac{1}{20}$ (5 percent) of the Earth's land surface.

Scientists describe a wetland as an area where water is at the surface of the soil or covering the soil for at least part of the year, including the time of year when wetland plants are growing. Lakes and rivers deeper than 6 feet are not included as wetlands because typical wetland plants are not found in water that deep. Some wetland animals such as ducks and fish, however, may swim into these deep-water areas.

Wetlands occur all over the world on every continent. They were once thought to be wastelands full of smelly, muddy ooze and dirty water, good only for breeding mosquitoes. Many wetland areas were drained of water or filled in so that the land could be used for growing food crops and building roads and homes. We now know that wetlands are important in many ways. Wetland plants clean water of dirt and chemicals. Some wetlands protect areas from flooding by acting like sponges, storing water when there is lots of rain or melting snow, and releasing the water slowly into streams and rivers. And people all over the world depend upon the fish, waterfowl, and other animals found in wetlands for their food.

Some wetland plants need to be in or on the water to survive. They are described as *emergent*, *submerged*, or *floating* plants. Examples of emergent plants are **cattails** and **water lilies**. They begin growing underwater with their roots in the wet soil, eventually growing above the water's surface. Submerged plants such as **hornwort** (or **coontail**, because it looks like a raccoon's tail) and some **pondweeds** spend their whole life underwater. They may or may not have their roots in the soil. **Duckweed** and the introduced, or non-native, **water hyacinth** are floating plants whose roots hang down from the water's surface. All these plants provide shade and protection for frogs, snails, small fish, and other aquatic animals. Ducks and other waterfowl also eat many of them.

The best-known wetland animal is probably the mosquito. About 3,000 different kinds of mosquitoes occur in the world, and they all need water to survive. Mosquitoes lay their eggs on or near water, and young mosquitoes stay underwater until they become adults. While they are in the water, they are a very important food for other wetland animals including fish, aquatic insects, and some birds.

Many animals depend upon wetlands. But one of the most amazing stories is about the millions of waterfowl that use wetlands as places to rest, eat, and raise their young. Each spring, birds that live in wetlands as far away as southern Asia, South America, and Africa fly north to breed at the wetlands along the Arctic Ocean in Europe, Asia, and North America. As they travel, sometimes for thousands of miles, they stop to rest and feed at wetlands along the way. Then, in the late summer and fall, after they've raised their young, they fly south again.

Amazing plants can also be found in wetlands. **Sphagnum moss** is a low green-and-brown plant that is common in bogs and fens. An incredible thing about this plant is that it can hold up to ten times its weight in water—just like a sponge. As you walk across sphagnum, it kind of bounces as water squeezes out and wets your shoes.

Wetlands are amazing places. Wear your boots and watch where you step as you enjoy learning about the plants and animals that live here.

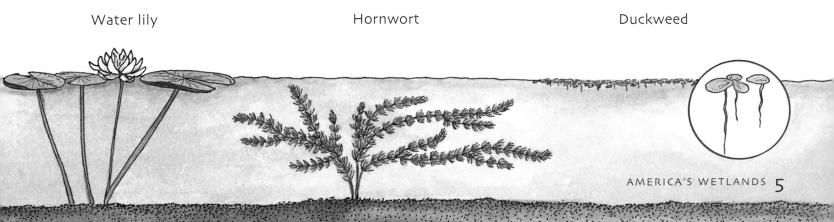

Water lily   Hornwort   Duckweed

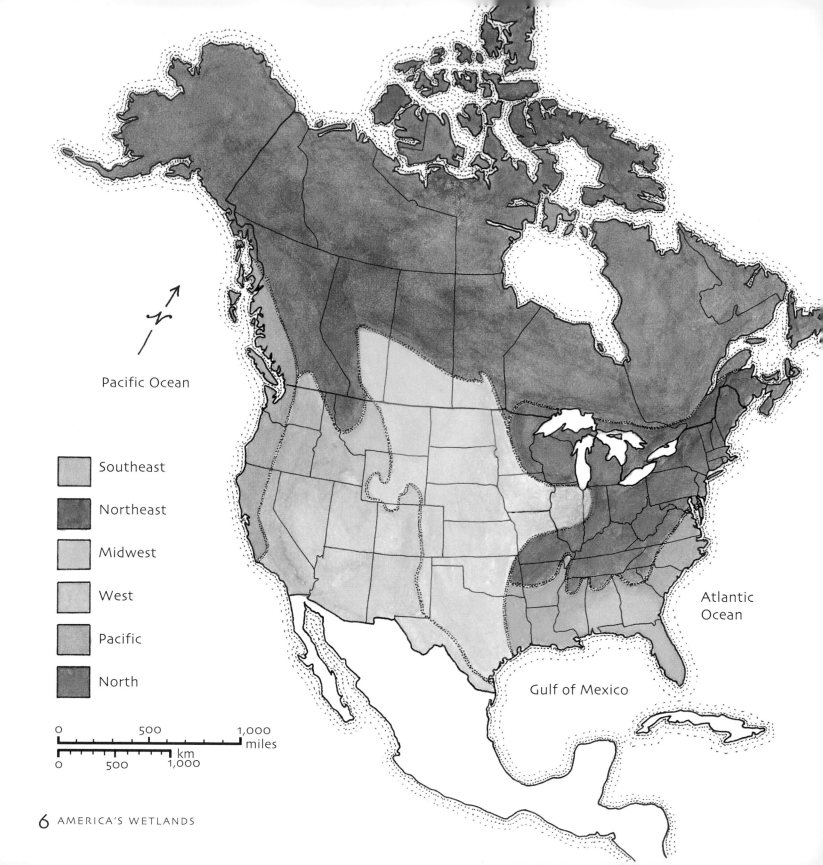

Pacific Ocean

Southeast

Northeast

Midwest

West

Pacific

North

0	500	1,000
		miles

0	500	1,000
		km

Atlantic Ocean

Gulf of Mexico

North American Wetlands

Wetlands can be found all over North America. This book covers the wetlands of six regions north of Mexico: Southeast, Northeast, Midwest, West, Pacific, and North. (Note: Although ponds, lakes, rivers, and streams are not considered wetlands by scientists, they have been included here because many wetland species live alongside or nearby these areas.)

Many types of wetlands, such as swamps, marshes, or ponds, occur in many different regions. But the plants and animals that live in these similar wetland habitats are often different, depending upon which region you are in. For example, even though a wetland may have trees and be called a **swamp**, the Atlantic white cedar swamp of the Northeast will have different plants and animals than the bald cypress swamp of the Southeast. And the ponds and shallow lakes of the North are temporary homes to many migrating birds each summer, while a desert pond in the West may only have a few bird species.

Some animals, especially birds that migrate such as **sandhill cranes** and **white pelicans**, will not be seen in an area year-round. Like many other wading birds and waterfowl, they are commonly seen for a few weeks in the spring and fall during migration. Sometimes you will not see an animal because it is hiding. The **American bittern** is common but hides among the rushes and other plants at the marshy edges of some wetlands. The color of this bird makes it even harder to find. Its striped brown and whitish feathers match the brown and light colors of the plant stems found where the bittern lives.

American bittern

Remember that wetland plants and animals live above *and below* the water. Some common turtles such as **snapping turtles** and **mud turtles** rarely leave the water or the muddy bottom. And many aquatic insects, like the **diving beetle**, spend most of their time underwater. Use this book to identify those wetland plants and animals that you're able to see along the shore of ponds, rivers, and lakes, and from trails and boardwalks along bogs and swamps.

Not all of the plants and animals on the two-page drawings will be found in each region all year long. But you will see many of them if you look closely and visit at different times of the year. Enjoy learning about the plants and animals of our North American wetlands.

Diving beetle

North American Wetlands

Wetland plants and animals may have different needs and will only be found in specific habitat areas. The cross section on these two pages will give you an idea of the types of habitats and some of the species that will be found there.

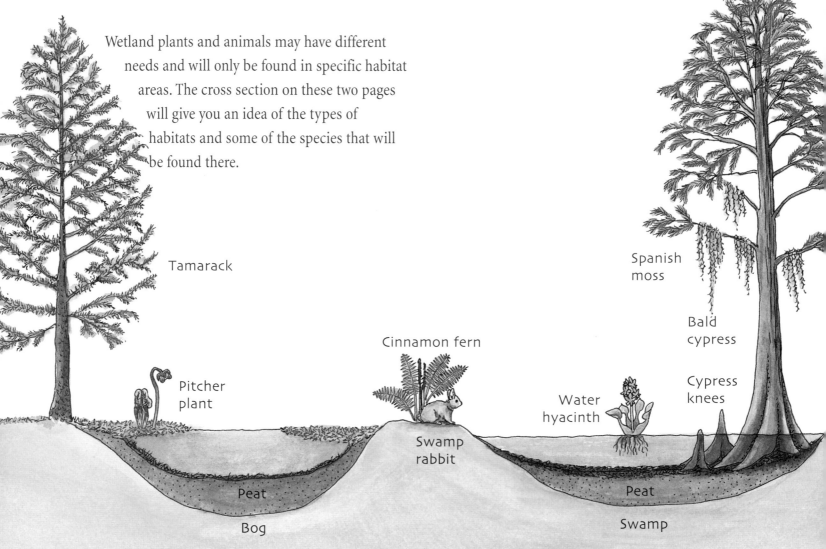

Tamarack

Pitcher plant

Cinnamon fern

Swamp rabbit

Peat

Bog

Spanish moss

Bald cypress

Cypress knees

Water hyacinth

Peat

Swamp

Bog—
A **bog** is often covered with a mat of sphagnum moss that makes the surface look like solid ground. But beware: you can sink through to the water below and into the mucky layer of decaying plants, called peat. **Black spruce** and **tamarack** grow along the bogs of the north, and **pitcher plants** are common farther south.

Marsh—
The most common wetland type in North America is the **marsh**. Grasses grow out of the shallow water and the ground is always soggy. Marshy areas can also be found along the edges of rivers, ponds, and lakes. **Marsh wrens** and **red-winged blackbirds** are two common birds that live among the marsh grasses.

Canada goose

Sky—

The **sky** is not a habitat, but many wetland birds, especially waterfowl, will be found here. Thousands of migrating ducks and geese may be seen and heard as they fly above the wetlands.

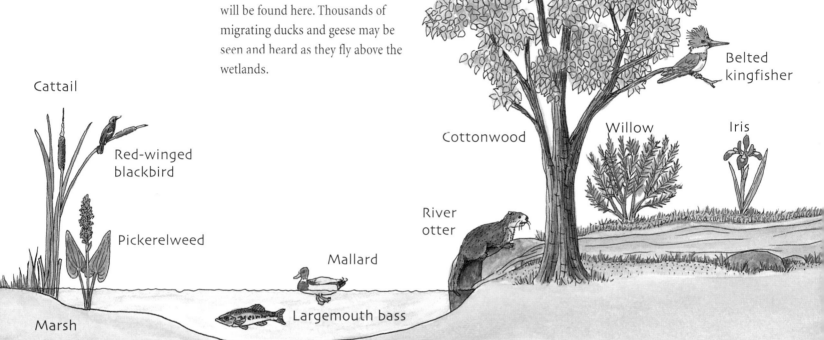

Cattail

Red-winged blackbird

Pickerelweed

Marsh

Belted kingfisher

Cottonwood

Willow

Iris

River otter

Mallard

Largemouth bass

Ponds and Lakes—

Aquatic plants and animals such as **snails**, **frogs**, and **crayfish** may be found along the swallow edges or muddy bottom, and the deeper areas are used by fish and waterfowl.

Swamp—

A place that has trees or shrubs and is almost always soggy or covered with at least a few inches of water is a **swamp**. Blackwater and brownwater swamps have water colored dark brown by underwater decaying leaves and other plant material. As these underwater rotting plants sink to the bottom, they create a spongy layer called **peat**. **Spanish moss** hangs from the trees in some swamps of the Southeast.

Streams and Rivers—

Willow shrubs and **cottonwood** trees are common alongside many streams and rivers, while fish, such as **brook trout**, may be found in the water. **Kingfishers**, a type of bird, live in burrows along the streambank. But you may notice them sitting on branches above the water's edge looking for a small fish to catch and eat.

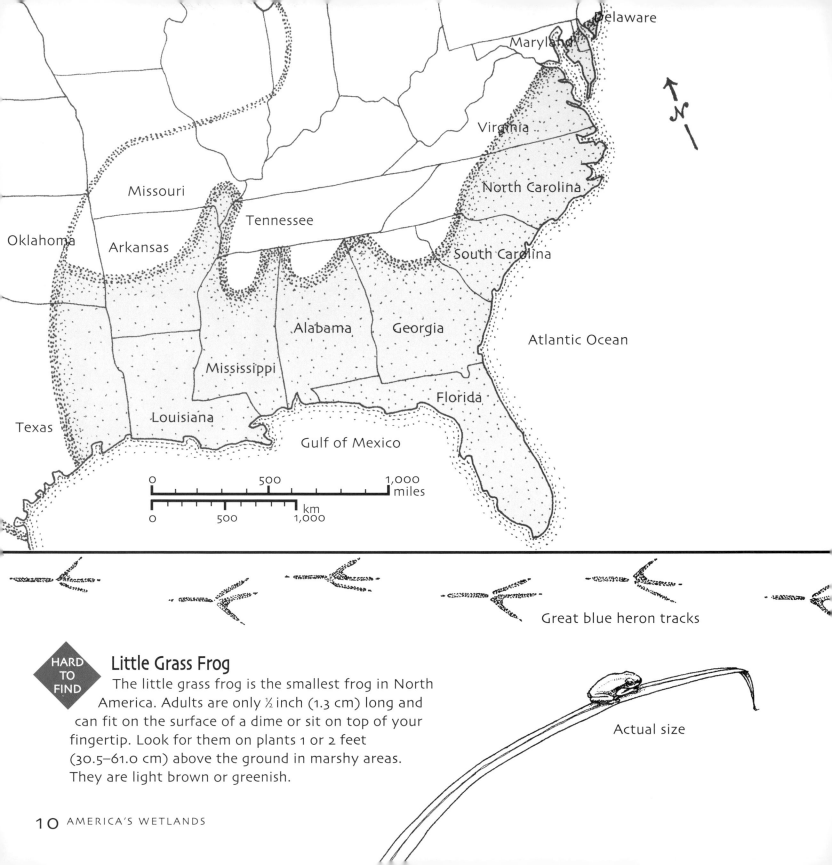

Delaware

Maryland

Virginia

Missouri

Tennessee

North Carolina

Oklahoma

Arkansas

South Carolina

Texas

Alabama

Georgia

Mississippi

Atlantic Ocean

Louisiana

Florida

Gulf of Mexico

| 0 | 500 | 1,000 miles |

| 0 | 500 | 1,000 km |

Great blue heron tracks

Little Grass Frog

HARD TO FIND

The little grass frog is the smallest frog in North America. Adults are only ½ inch (1.3 cm) long and can fit on the surface of a dime or sit on top of your fingertip. Look for them on plants 1 or 2 feet (30.5–61.0 cm) above the ground in marshy areas. They are light brown or greenish.

Actual size

Southeast

A boat ride through the swamps and bayous of the Southeast is a great way to see these impressive wetlands. Look up as you glide past **cypress** and **tupelo gum** trees. You'll probably see Spanish moss hanging like thick greenish gray hair from the tree branches. Spanish moss is actually not a moss, but a type of **air plant**, which means that the plant gets its water from the air instead of through roots in the ground. Snakes are a part of swamps and bayous too. Maybe you'll spot the **rat snake** in the branches of trees and shrubs as it hunts for eggs in birds' nests.

Unusual sounds drift across the water in some southeastern swamps and marshes. One is a sort of rumbling, booming noise that goes on for a few seconds. That is the sound of male **alligators** in the spring, protecting their territory and trying to attract females. Other sounds might remind you of two rocks clicking together or grunting pigs. The clicking sound comes from the tiny **cricket frog**, one of the most common frogs in the area; the grunting is the call of the large **pig frog**, a type of bullfrog. Both frogs hide among plants at the water's edge or among the floating **water lily** pads.

Alligators dig holes in the peat and mud of swamps and marshy areas. These **'gator holes** are usually hidden underwater. But during the dry season when the water level of the surrounding area has gone down, they may be the only places with water still available. At the 'gator holes, look for **egrets** and **herons** hoping to catch trapped fish. Other animals may also come to drink the water or hunt for food. But remember: an alligator dug the hole and could still be using it. Be careful.

Some of the plants of the swamps have more than one common name. **Sweet pepperbush** also goes by the name **poor-man's soap**. Take a wet leaf and rub it between your hands. You will create a lather that you can use as soap. Another common plant is **fetterbush**, a shrub with thorny branches that grows in dense thickets. Fetterbush's other name is **hurrah bush**, because when you finally make your way through a group of these shrubs you'll probably shout, "hurrah!"

A pretty and common floating plant in the Southeast is the introduced (non-native) **water hyacinth**, a fast-growing plant with purple flowers and bright-green leaves. Water hyacinths multiply so quickly that they can clog waterways and shade out the sunlight needed by plants that live underwater.

One of the most famous wetlands in the Southeast is Everglades National Park. This is a huge marsh of very slow-moving water in southern Florida. **Saw grass**, a grasslike plant with tiny teeth along its edge, grows out of the shallow water and covers the area for miles in all directions.

A visit to these incredible wetlands will be an experience you will never forget.

SOUTHEAST

Bald cypress

Spanish moss

Barred owl

Pond pine

Green d

Pileated woodpecker

Buttonbush

American alligator

Great blue heron

Golden club

Wood duck

Red-winged blackbird

Double-crested cormorant

Spatterdock

Anhinga

Water hyacinth

Prothonotary warbler

Cottonmouth

Green a

Rough green snake

Cooter

Fetterbush

Pond slider

Garter snake

Crayfish

Chain fern

Water tupelo

Overcup oak

Cinnamon fern

Loblolly bay

Belted kingfisher

Red maple

Raccoon

Great egret

Titi

White ibis

Grass-pink

Pitcher plant

Swamp rabbit

Little blue heron

Common moorhen

Palamedes swallowtail

Pipewort

Fishing spider

Water lily

Pickerelweed

Leopard frog

Largemouth bass

Mosquitofish

Gar

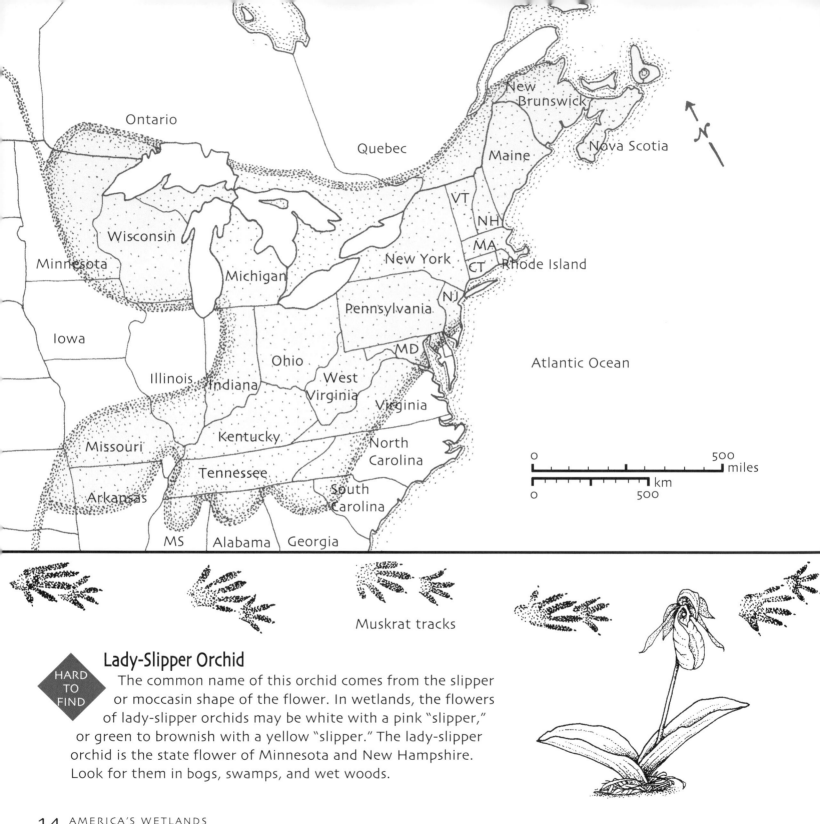

Muskrat tracks

Lady-Slipper Orchid

HARD TO FIND

The common name of this orchid comes from the slipper or moccasin shape of the flower. In wetlands, the flowers of lady-slipper orchids may be white with a pink "slipper," or green to brownish with a yellow "slipper." The lady-slipper orchid is the state flower of Minnesota and New Hampshire. Look for them in bogs, swamps, and wet woods.

Northeast

The northeastern part of North America has many bogs and fens. You can also find **muskegs** here. Muskegs are bogs with spruce trees, and they are unusual because very few plants normally grow in bogs.

Sphagnum moss

One plant that is common in bogs is **sphagnum moss,** which often covers the entire surface of a small pond and makes it look like solid ground. But as you begin to walk across the sphagnum, your feet start to sink and water creeps up around your shoes or ankles. In some cases, people have slipped through the sphagnum layer and fallen into the deeper water below.

Bogs and fens look similar. They are both pools of water with sphagnum moss growing out from the shore. But bogs are where you should look for carnivorous plants such as **pitcher plants** and **sundews**. Bog water lacks nutrients, and that means these types of plants can't get their food from the water or soil like other plants do. Bog water comes from rain and is acidic—something many plants and animals don't like. So carnivorous plants *catch* their own food by attracting and trapping insects.

By comparison, fen water is nutritious. Fen water flows in from the surrounding land area, on the surface or underground, washing nutrients into the fen. The water is also much less acidic so you'll find many more types of plants here. Look for **bayberry bushes, dwarf birch, bulrush,** and **horsetail** in fens.

As the weather warms up after winter, listen for the sounds at night near **vernal pools**. These shallow ponds fill up with rain or melted snow in the spring and attract many frogs, turtles, and other wetland animals. If you hear bells jingling, that is the chorus of little brown treefrogs, called **spring peepers**. Loud quacking sounds at night probably come from the **wood frog**, another brown frog. And if you hear a soft, high-pitched whine, then you better be wearing long sleeves and insect repellent because that's the sound of a **mosquito**. All three of these animals lay eggs in and around vernal pools.

Spring peeper and wood frog

Beavers are common in this region, and you might even spot a **black bear** among the **black gum** (also called **black tupelo**) trees or eating the **highbush blueberries**.

Three other regions—North, Midwest, and Southeast—border the Northeast region. If you're near one of these other regions, you'll probably see plants and animals common to those areas too.

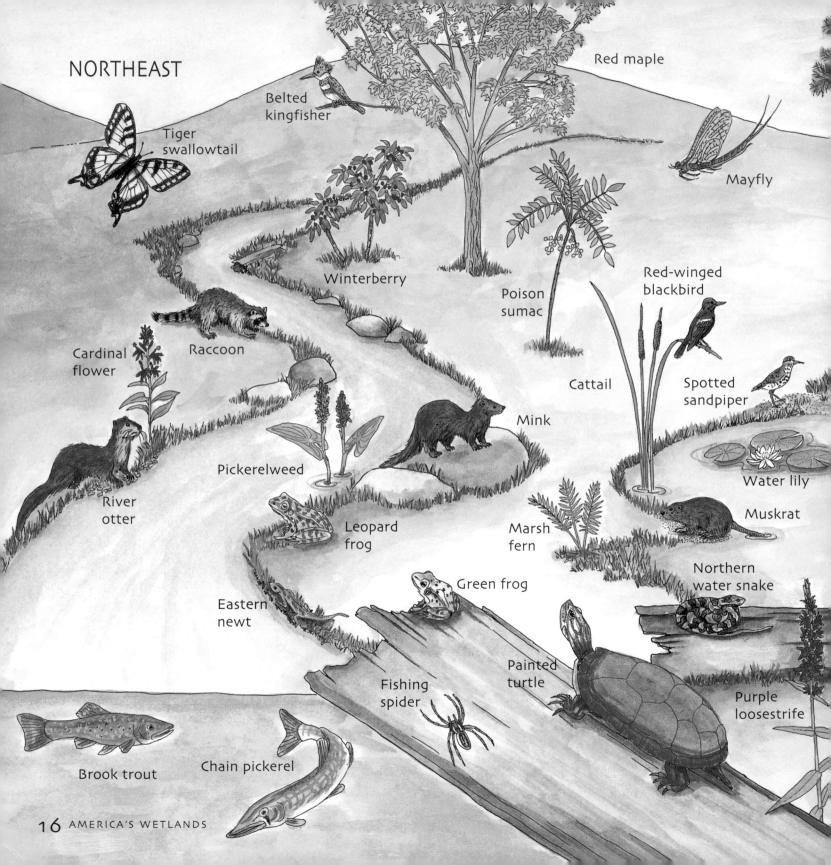

NORTHEAST

Belted kingfisher

Red maple

Tiger swallowtail

Mayfly

Winterberry

Poison sumac

Red-winged blackbird

Raccoon

Cardinal flower

Cattail

Spotted sandpiper

Pickerelweed

Mink

River otter

Water lily

Marsh fern

Muskrat

Leopard frog

Eastern newt

Green frog

Northern water snake

Fishing spider

Painted turtle

Purple loosestrife

Brook trout

Chain pickerel

Herring gull

Common reed

Atlantic white cedar

Wild rice

Iris

Skunk cabbage

Lotus

Joe-pye weed

Arrowhead

Beaver and lodge

Common loon

Mallard

Pond lily

Common goldeneye

Canada goose

Black duck

Highbush blueberry

Bog rosemary

Pitcher plant

Grass-pink

Cranberry

Ribbon snake

Labrador tea

Leatherleaf

Swamp rose

Bog laurel

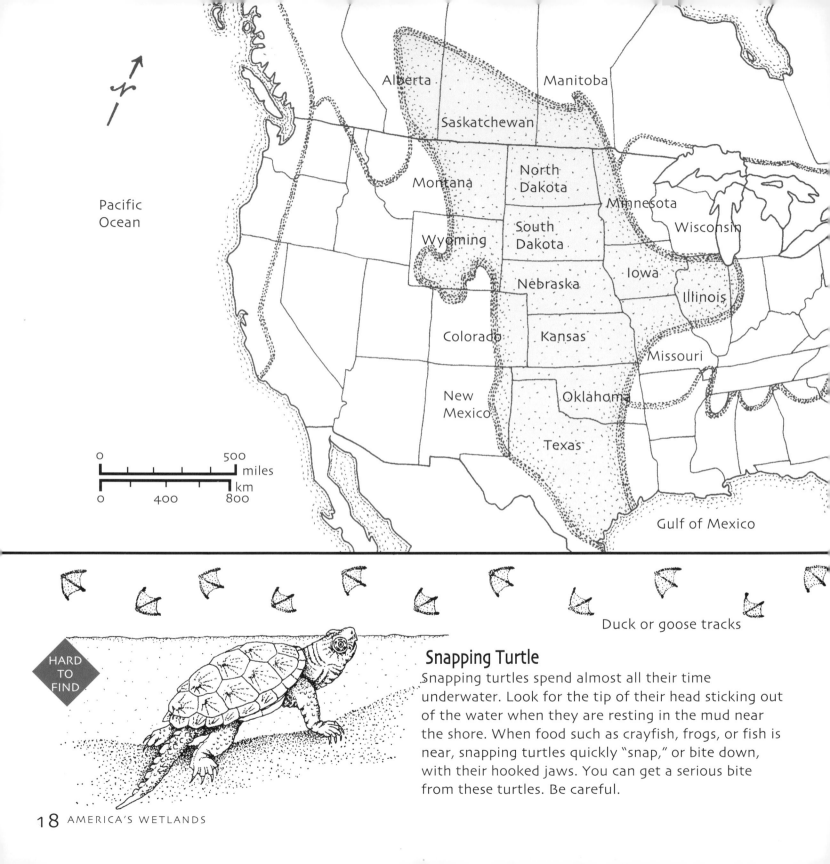

Pacific
Ocean

Alberta

Manitoba

Saskatchewan

Montana

North
Dakota

Minnesota

Wisconsin

Wyoming

South
Dakota

Iowa

Nebraska

Illinois

Colorado

Kansas

Missouri

New
Mexico

Oklahoma

Texas

Gulf of Mexico

0   500
         miles
         km
0   400   800

Duck or goose tracks

HARD
TO
FIND

Snapping Turtle

Snapping turtles spend almost all their time underwater. Look for the tip of their head sticking out of the water when they are resting in the mud near the shore. When food such as crayfish, frogs, or fish is near, snapping turtles quickly "snap," or bite down, with their hooked jaws. You can get a serious bite from these turtles. Be careful.

Midwest

The Midwest is one of the major migration routes for birds in North America. Most of the **sandhill cranes** in the world fly north through the Midwest. And more than 7 million **ducks** and **geese** also use the marshes, ponds, rivers, and lakes when they head north in the spring. All in all, more than one-third of all migrating birds on the continent will rest, eat, raise their young, or somehow use this region.

Many of the migrating ducks and geese will stay in the wetlands of the **Prairie Pothole Region** for the summer. These wetlands were created when glaciers dug holes in the earth as they moved across the ground. At the end of the last ice age, 10,000 to 12,000 years ago, huge chunks of ice were left behind. The ice chunks melted to form millions of ponds and lakes called **prairie potholes** and **kettleholes** that are usually filled with water from rain and melting snow.

The Prairie Pothole Region originally had about 25 million separate wetland areas. But many were filled in and leveled for growing crops or grazing cattle. As of the 1980s, about 8–11 million of these water areas were still there. Up to 70 percent of the ducks and geese born in North America are born in the Midwest. And almost all of those are from the Prairie Pothole Region. That is why this area is called "the duck factory" of North America.

Farther south is a group of wetlands called **Cheyenne Bottoms**. There you'll find open water, mudflats, marshy areas, and a wet meadow. Look for an **avocet** swishing its bill in the water trying to stir up food. A large gray hawk flying low across the meadow is probably a **northern harrier** looking for frogs to catch and eat. You may even see the endangered **whooping cranes** stop and rest on their way farther south to spend the winter on the coast of Texas. These large white birds are more than 4 feet (1.2 m) tall with black legs and red feathers on their heads. When they fly, look for the black wing tips.

Whooping crane

Cottonwood trees, with dark trunks and bright-green leaves, grow along the rivers, and **willow shrubs** sometimes grow right at the water's edge. Look closely along the shore in the early morning or late afternoon to spot a **coyote** or **raccoon** coming to the water for a drink. And in the calm water of slow-moving rivers and shallow lakes you may see the head of a swimming turtle or the movement of tiny fish such as the **brook stickleback**.

Although looking for ducks and other waterfowl is a good reason to visit the Midwest, the many kinds of wetland life will keep you coming back.

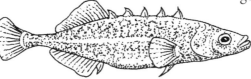

Brook stickleback

MIDWEST

Belted kingfisher

Silver maple

Cottonwood

Willow

Yellow-headed blackbird

Sycamore

Cinnamon fern

Iris

Great blue heron

Raccoon

Beaver

Bur reed

Wild rice

Cardinal flower

Monkey flower

Avocet

Coot

Massasauga

Garter snake

20

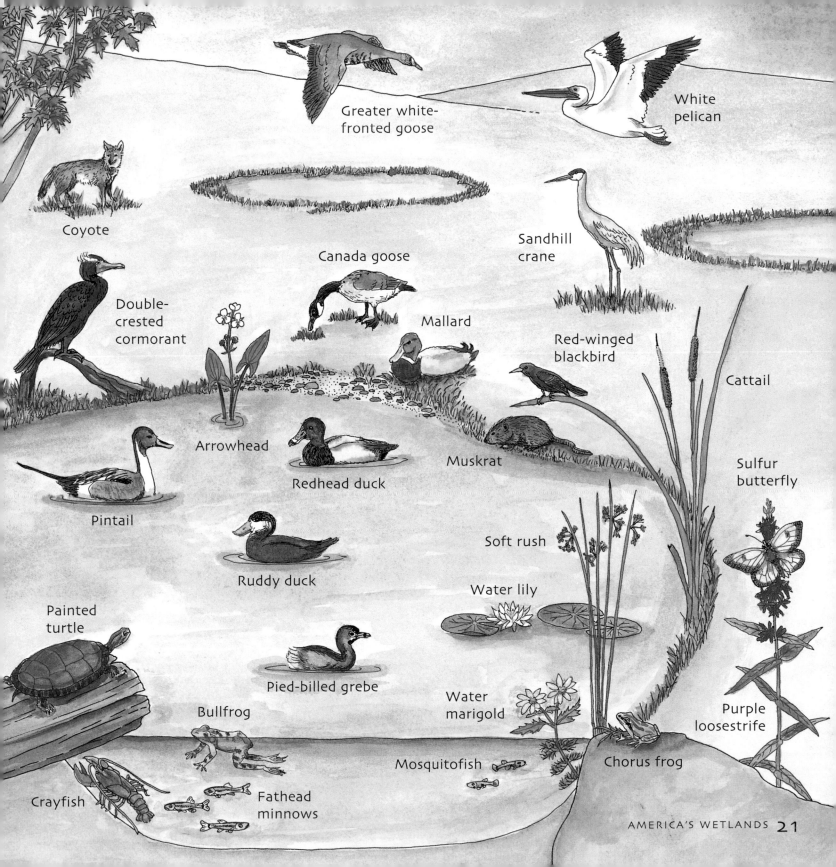

Greater white-fronted goose

White pelican

Coyote

Sandhill crane

Canada goose

Double-crested cormorant

Mallard

Red-winged blackbird

Cattail

Arrowhead

Redhead duck

Muskrat

Sulfur butterfly

Pintail

Soft rush

Ruddy duck

Water lily

Painted turtle

Pied-billed grebe

Water marigold

Purple loosestrife

Bullfrog

Chorus frog

Mosquitofish

Crayfish

Fathead minnows

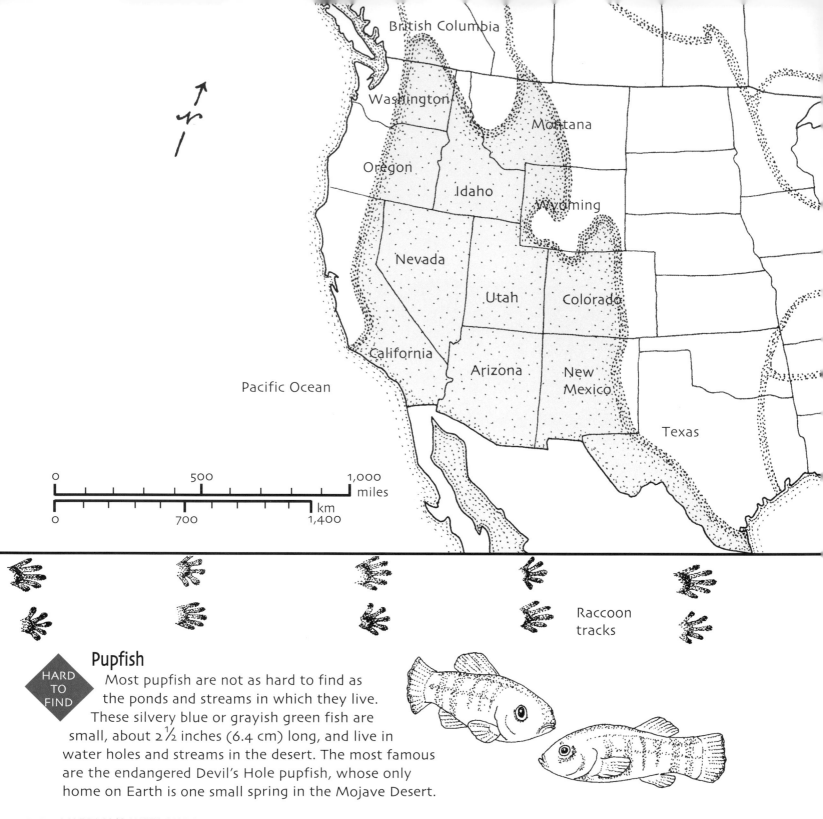

British Columbia

Washington

Montana

Oregon

Idaho

Wyoming

Nevada

Utah

Colorado

California

Arizona

New Mexico

Pacific Ocean

Texas

| 0 | 500 | 1,000 miles |

| 0 | 700 | 1,400 km |

Raccoon tracks

Pupfish

HARD TO FIND

Most pupfish are not as hard to find as the ponds and streams in which they live. These silvery blue or grayish green fish are small, about 2½ inches (6.4 cm) long, and live in water holes and streams in the desert. The most famous are the endangered Devil's Hole pupfish, whose only home on Earth is one small spring in the Mojave Desert.

West

In much of western North America, huge areas of desert or other dry regions often separate rivers, lakes, and marshy areas. Wetland plants and animals will be concentrated in these wet areas, and your chances of seeing them are very good.

Rain in the desert can make temporary shallow lakes out of low-lying areas called **playas**. You may not find many plants growing in playas, but they are good places to look for **northern pintails**, **sandhill cranes**, **American coots**, and other water birds.

Rain or melting snow can also create **vernal pools**, most common in the coastal areas and mountain foothills of California. As the water in these shallow pools slowly evaporates, flowers grow at the water's edge creating rings of color. When the pools first begin to dry up, white **meadowfoam** appears. As the water becomes more shallow, a ring of yellow **goldfields** will bloom and the center of the pool may be covered with purple **downingia**. In the water that is left, **tadpoles** and **fairy shrimp** that hatched from eggs laid the previous year must grow into adults and mate before the pool dries up completely. That way, a new batch of eggs will be ready to hatch after the next year's rains.

Grebe on a nest of smartweed

The Great Salt Lake in Utah and the Salton Sea in southern California are large salty lakes that attract thousands of birds. Many of these birds, such as **white pelicans**, **Canada geese**, and **greater white-fronted geese** may only be there during spring or fall migration.

Hard-stem bulrush (often called **tule** in the western United States) and **cattails** are common plants of shallow marshes and sloughs. Birds hide and nest among these shore plants. Another shallow-water plant is called **smartweed**. Grebes weave the stems into floating nests and waterfowl eat the seeds.

Late spring and early summer are the best times to find flowers along the streams and marshy edges of lakes in the western mountains. Purple **swamp onions** (crush a leaf—it smells like onion!) and **bog orchids** with tiny white flowers grow where the ground is wet. In the slow water of shallow mountain streams, look for **brown trout** swimming against the current. And if you're lucky, you'll see a gray bird hopping among the rocks and in the water of a fast-moving mountain stream. That's a **dipper**, the only songbird that swims underwater.

Just because the West is a mostly dry part of North America does not mean it has no wetlands. You may have to look a bit harder to find them, but it's worth it.

Meadowfoam

Goldfields

Downingia

Fairy shrimp

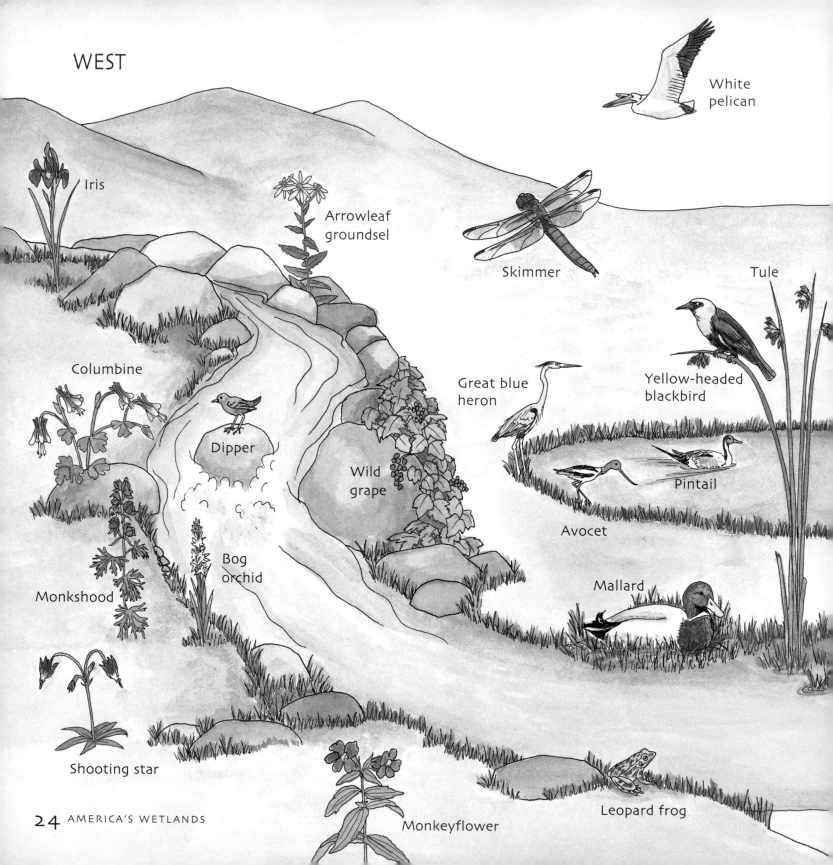

WEST

White pelican

Iris

Arrowleaf groundsel

Skimmer

Tule

Columbine

Great blue heron

Yellow-headed blackbird

Dipper

Wild grape

Avocet

Pintail

Monkshood

Bog orchid

Mallard

Shooting star

Monkeyflower

Leopard frog

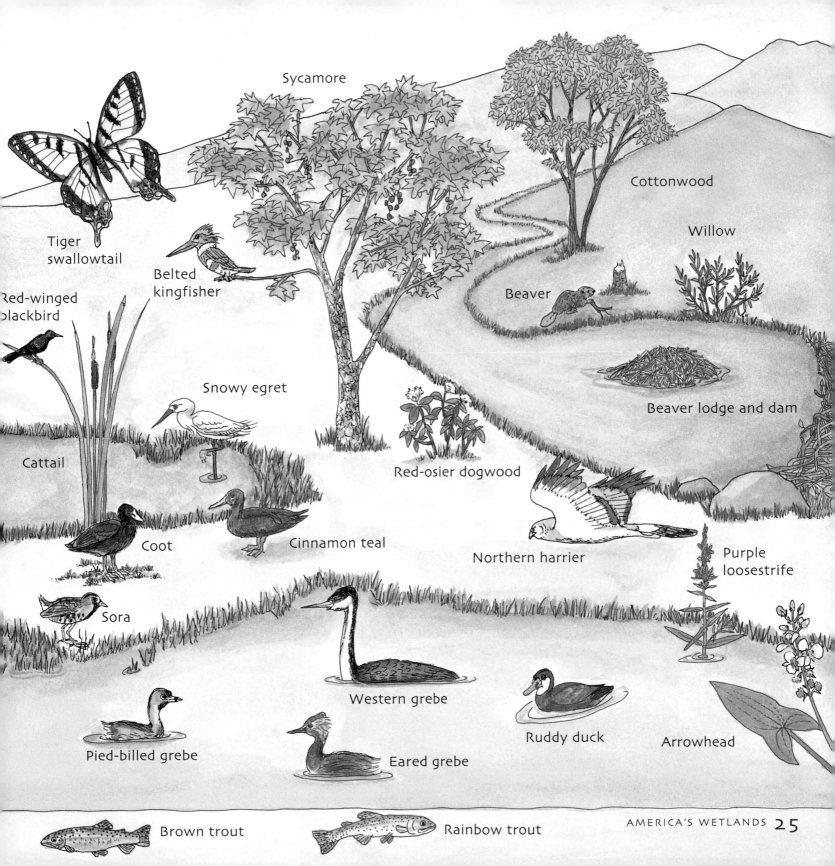

Sycamore

Cottonwood

Willow

Tiger swallowtail

Belted kingfisher

Beaver

Red-winged blackbird

Snowy egret

Beaver lodge and dam

Cattail

Red-osier dogwood

Coot

Cinnamon teal

Northern harrier

Purple loosestrife

Sora

Western grebe

Ruddy duck

Arrowhead

Pied-billed grebe

Eared grebe

Brown trout

Rainbow trout

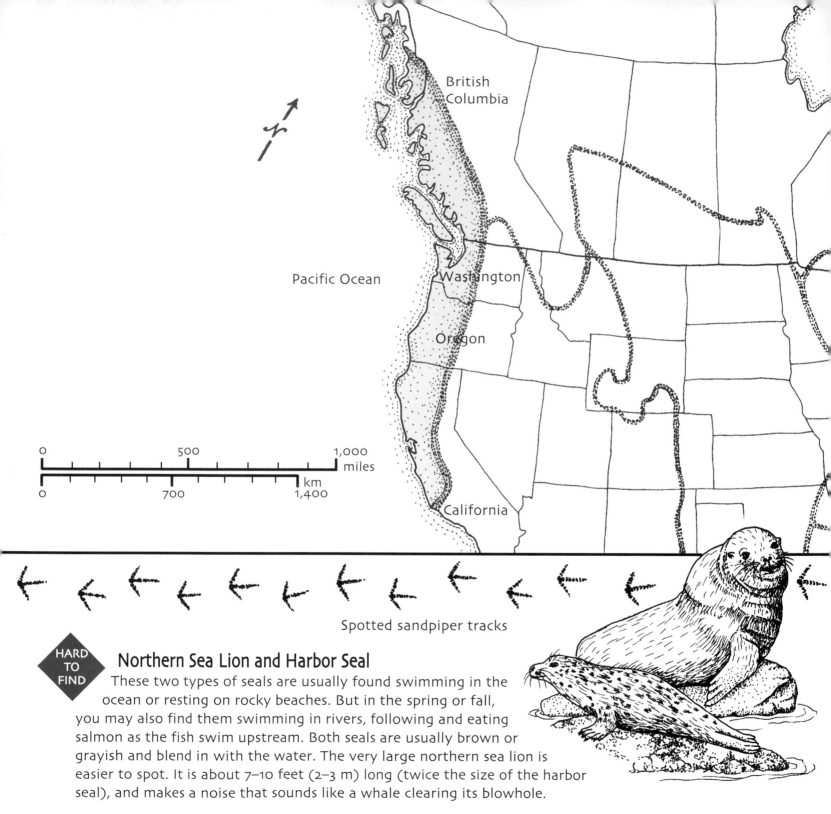

British Columbia

Pacific Ocean

Washington

Oregon

California

0		500		1,000 miles

| 0 | | 700 | | 1,400 km |

Spotted sandpiper tracks

Northern Sea Lion and Harbor Seal

HARD TO FIND

These two types of seals are usually found swimming in the ocean or resting on rocky beaches. But in the spring or fall, you may also find them swimming in rivers, following and eating salmon as the fish swim upstream. Both seals are usually brown or grayish and blend in with the water. The very large northern sea lion is easier to spot. It is about 7–10 feet (2–3 m) long (twice the size of the harbor seal), and makes a noise that sounds like a whale clearing its blowhole.

Pacific

Rain and lots of foggy, cloudy days help keep this region along the Pacific Ocean wet and green. From 50–140 inches (1.3–3.6 m) of rain fall in some areas each year. You may be surprised to learn that a rain forest also occurs here. Although not a wetland, this cool-temperature, or temperate, rain forest has trees such as the **western red cedar** and **western hemlock**. Those same trees are also found alongside the area's wetland ponds and bogs.

Migrating ducks, geese, and other waterfowl are common. Some come to the Pacific region from the south and stay through the summer. Other waterfowl spend the winter here and fly farther north when the weather warms up in the spring. Still others, such as **mallard ducks** and **Canada geese**, can be found here all year long.

Look across a wet meadow or bog in April and May and you may see the purple-flowering **camas**. This hard-to-miss plant is related to onions and was eaten by Native Americans.

Western hemlock

Salmon are in the streams and rivers of this area if you visit at the right time of year. Young salmon, or fry, hatch from eggs in inland streams during late winter or early spring. The fry hide among the rocks and dead branches in the water and eat the insects that live underwater among the plants near the shore. Some types of salmon will live in the streams and rivers for up to one and a half years. Sockeye salmon migrate to lakes where they spend the first year or two of their life. But eventually almost all salmon travel downstream to the sea. Within a few years, the salmon return to the freshwater streams and rivers where they were born to mate, lay eggs, and die.

Western pond turtles sun themselves along the shores of ponds and other shallow waters in the southern part of this region. (Western pond turtles are rare in some areas. Please do not disturb them or pick them up.) Look for these turtles in wetland areas that have lots of plants growing out of and alongside the water.

Wet meadows, bogs, and dark, shady forests of tall trees are all found here. Prepare for cool, wet weather and enjoy these wetlands.

Western pond turtle

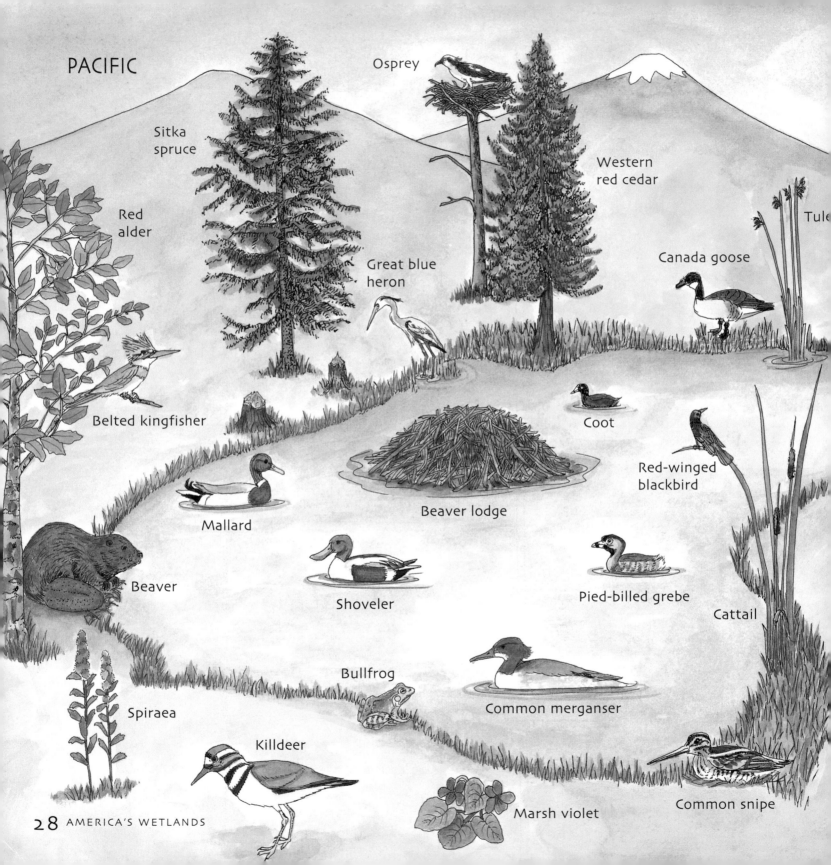

PACIFIC

Osprey

Sitka spruce

Western red cedar

Red alder

Tule

Canada goose

Great blue heron

Belted kingfisher

Coot

Red-winged blackbird

Beaver lodge

Mallard

Beaver

Shoveler

Pied-billed grebe

Cattail

Bullfrog

Spiraea

Common merganser

Killdeer

Marsh violet

Common snipe

Bald eagle

Lorquin's admiral

Tiger swallowtail

Cottonwood

Camas

Willow

Devil's club

Dipper

Northern harrier

Cobra lily

Ash

River otter

Raccoon

Bog orchid

Spotted sandpiper

Red-osier dogwood

Soft rush

Sockeye salmon

Rainbow trout

Pacific treefrog

29

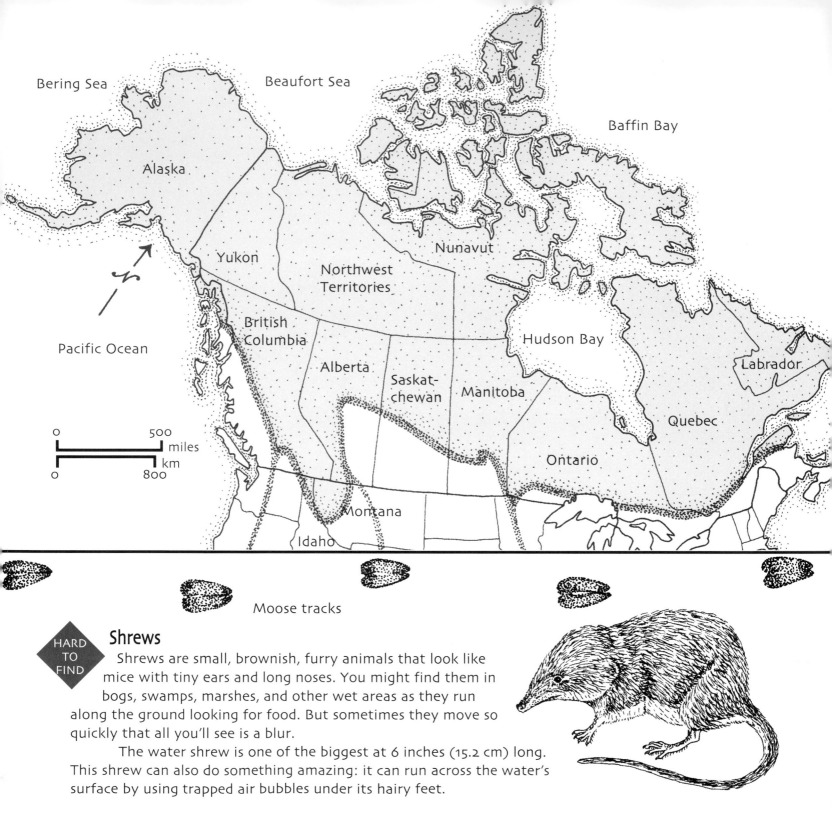

Bering Sea

Beaufort Sea

Baffin Bay

Alaska

Yukon

Nunavut

Northwest
Territories

Pacific Ocean

British
Columbia

Hudson Bay

Alberta

Saskat-
chewan

Manitoba

Labrador

Quebec

0   500
|————————| miles
|————————| km
0   800

Ontario

Montana

Idaho

Moose tracks

Shrews

HARD TO FIND

Shrews are small, brownish, furry animals that look like mice with tiny ears and long noses. You might find them in bogs, swamps, marshes, and other wet areas as they run along the ground looking for food. But sometimes they move so quickly that all you'll see is a blur.

The water shrew is one of the biggest at 6 inches (15.2 cm) long. This shrew can also do something amazing: it can run across the water's surface by using trapped air bubbles under its hairy feet.

North

The land in the far north is covered in snow and ice most of the year. For a few months in late spring and during the summer, however, the surface snow and ice melt creating ponds, lakes, marshes, bogs, and swamps. But a few feet below the surface, the ground stays frozen. This permafrost prevents all the melted snow and ice from being absorbed. So huge areas stay wet and soggy.

These wetlands are very important to many waterfowl of North America and to birds from other continents as well. They come here to breed, nest (lay eggs), and raise their young. The **Canada goose**, **snow goose**, and **tundra swan** can all be found here. At least fifteen different species of ducks and four types of grebes can also be found here during the warmer weather.

The mammals of this area include the **musk ox** and two types of **caribou**. The musk ox is related to the **bison**, or **buffalo**, of the Great Plains and is found in the wetlands of the far North close to the Arctic Ocean.

Caribou are related to deer, moose, and elk. They move as herds across large areas in the North. Both types of caribou live together in the winter. But in the summer time, the **barren ground caribou** head north to the tundra and the **woodland caribou** head to the boggy muskegs farther south. Both the musk ox and the caribou eat plants.

Carnivores, or meat eaters, such as the **arctic fox** and **mink**, can also be found here. They hunt and eat the birds that migrate to the wetlands each year and also eat shrews, mice, voles, and other small animals.

You may see what look like white cotton balls waving in the breeze. Those are the hairy seed heads of **cotton grass**. It is a common plant found in wet meadows, marshes, bogs, muskegs, and also on the tundra of the far north.

The northern part of North America has some of the most natural remaining wetlands. Many areas are wilderness, unchanged by people. There are few roads and travel through the area is not easy, but if you have a chance to visit these unspoiled bogs, marshes, swamps, and ponds, go! Enjoy the adventure.

Snow goose
Dark form
Light form

Arctic fox

NORTH

Greater white-fronted goose

Tern

Arctic fritillary

Tundra swan

Snow goose

Caribou

Cattails

Water arum

Red-necked phalarope

Dragonfly

Cotton grass

Pintail

Horsetail

Yellowlegs

Smartweed

Horned grebe

Common loon

Muskrat

Spotted sandpiper

Pond lily

Mink

Northern pike

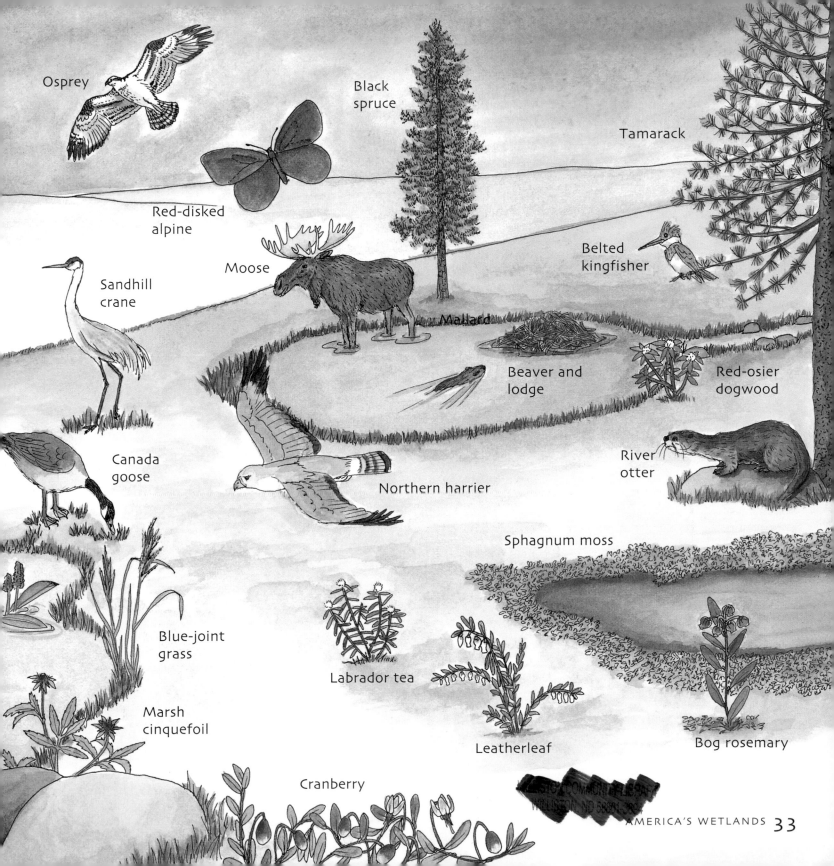

Osprey

Black spruce

Tamarack

Red-disked alpine

Moose

Belted kingfisher

Sandhill crane

Mallard

Beaver and lodge

Red-osier dogwood

Canada goose

River otter

Northern harrier

Sphagnum moss

Blue-joint grass

Labrador tea

Marsh cinquefoil

Leatherleaf

Bog rosemary

Cranberry

Common Plants and Animals

Some plants and animals are very common and can be found in more than one wetland area. For example, **cattails**, **mosquitoes**, and **Canada geese** are found in all six wetland regions.

Information next to the drawings will help you learn where to look and what to look for. Remember that the time of year and the time of day are important too. Some birds will only be in certain wetlands when they stop to rest and eat during spring and fall migration. Nocturnal animals are usually out only at night. And plants and animals that need a lot of water may only be found in an area after the rainy season has soaked the ground and filled the swamps, marshes, and ponds.

Some of the bird drawings only show the more color-ful and easier-to-spot males. Female birds often have plain colors that blend in with their habitat and help them hide while they're nesting and protecting their young.

Look closely at everything and everywhere. You may be amazed at what you will find.

CANADA GOOSE
Color: Tan body with black neck and white cheeks.
Size: 25–45 inches (64–114 cm) tall.
Food: Grasses and grasslike plants. Also wheat, corn, and other crop plants.
Notes: Canada geese are very common. Look for them on or near lakes and ponds. They fly in a **V**-formation when they're migrating.

MOSQUITO
Color: Brownish; many have dark and light bands on legs.
Size: About $\frac{1}{4}$ inch (0.6 cm) long.
Food: Adult females feed on blood; adult males drink plant nectar.
Notes: Mosquitoes breed in dirty or clean still water. Some species can spread disease. They are especially common near water during the warm weather of late spring and summer.

BEAVER
Color: Dark brown.
Size: Body 3–4 feet (0.9–1.2 m) long. Tail about 1 foot (0.3 m) long.
Food: Tree bark.
Notes: A flooded area with a dome-shaped island of sticks in the water is probably a beaver pond. The island is the beaver's home, or lodge. You may see beavers just before dark or very early in the morning. Look for a **V**-shaped line of ripples as the beaver swims with only its head above the water. The beaver is the state animal of New York and Oregon. It is also the national symbol of Canada.

CATTAIL

Color: Green leaves with brown hot dog–shaped bunches of tiny flowers.

Size: 3–9 feet (0.9–2.7 m) tall.

Notes: Cattails are found in all six wetland regions. Look for them along the edges of marshes and other shallow water.

DRAGONFLIES and DAMSELFLIES

Color: The green darner dragonfly has a green and bluish body. Many other dragonflies are different shades of brown. Bluet damselflies are blue or red.

Size: Dragonflies are usually 2–3 inches (5.0–7.6 cm) long. Damselflies are about 1–2 inches (2.5–5.0 cm) long.

Food: Adult dragonflies eat mosquitoes and other small flying insects. Adult damselflies eat small insects with soft bodies.

Notes: Look for these insects on bright, sunny days flying above the marshy edges of ponds and lakes or sitting on plants growing in or near the water. The green darner is the state insect of Washington.

MALLARD

Color: Male has a green head, a white ring around the neck, a brown breast, and tan body. Female has a tan head with a brown and tan body.

Size: 23 inches (58 cm) long.

Food: Mostly aquatic plants.

Notes: Mallards are a type of "dabbling" duck. This means they float on the water and tilt their heads underwater to eat while their tails stick up in the air. Look for the curl at the tip of the male's tail.

IRIS

Color: Bluish purple flower with green leaves.

Size: 2–3 feet (0.6–0.9 m) tall.

Notes: Look for irises in and around swamps and marshy areas. The iris is the state flower of Louisiana and Tennessee and the provincial flower of Quebec.

PIED-BILLED GREBE

Color: Brown.

Size: 13 inches (33 cm) long.

Food: Small aquatic animals.

Notes: Look in the water of marshy ponds and sloughs. Grebes dive underwater to look for food and then pop up to the surface in a different spot.

Birds

AMERICAN COOT

Color: Dark gray (looks black) with a white bill.
Size: 15 ½ inches (39 cm) long.
Food: Aquatic plants and small aquatic animals.
Notes: Can dive underwater to get food. Look for them in marshes or on lakes and ponds.

BELTED KINGFISHER

Color: Bluish gray with a white ring around the neck.
Size: 13 inches (33 cm) long with a head that seems too big for its body.
Food: Small fish.
Notes: Kingfishers sit on branches hanging over the edges of streams, rivers, and ponds. You may also see them dive headfirst—from a branch or from the air—into the water after a fish.

PINTAIL

Color: Male has a brown head, white breast, and grayish body with a long, narrow, black tail. Female is light brown with darker brown blotches.
Size: 21 inches (53 cm) long.
Food: Plants.
Notes: Look for the long, pointed black tail of the male to help identify the pintail as it floats on the water of ponds and lakes.

RED-WINGED BLACKBIRD

Color: Males are black with red shoulders edged in yellow; females are brown with white and brown streaks on their breast.
Size: 8–9 inches (20–23 cm) long.
Food: Insects and seeds.
Notes: Common in marshy areas. Red-winged blackbirds often sit on cattails or other plants at the water's edge.

WOOD DUCK

Color: The top of the male's head is green and the cheeks are black. White stripes on the cheek connect to white on the front of the neck and the breast is cinnamon brown. Female is grayish tan.
Size: 18 ½ inches (47 cm) long.
Food: Wood ducks eat mostly acorns from oak trees and seeds of wetland plants.
Notes: Wood ducks nest in holes of wetland trees or in nearby wooded areas. The colorful pattern of the males makes them easy to spot when they're swimming on the water. The wood duck is the state waterfowl of Mississippi.

SNOWY EGRET and GREAT EGRET

Color: White feathers, black legs. Snowy egret has a black bill; great egret has a yellow bill.
Size: The snowy egret is up to 2 feet (0.6 m) tall and the great egret is about 3 feet (1.0 m) tall.
Food: Mostly fish and other aquatic animals.
Notes: Look for them walking in the shallow edges of marshes and ponds. As the snowy egret walks, it swishes its yellow feet in the water to stir up the animals that it hunts for food. Snowy egrets are said to have "golden slippers" because of their yellow feet.

Arthropods (Insects and Their Relatives) and Snails

WHIRLIGIG BEETLE

Color: Black.
Size: $1/4$–$1/2$ inch (0.6–1.3 cm) long.
Food: Insects.
Notes: These beetles swim in whirling circles on the surface of ponds and still streams. Their eyes are divided into upper and lower portions. This allows them to look underwater and above the water at the same time.

SNAILS

Color: Brown or tan; some have bands of lighter or darker color on their shells.
Size: Up to $2 1/2$ inches (6.4 cm) long, but usually much smaller.
Food: Usually plants; some feed on dead animals.
Notes: Look in the mucky, muddy margins of ponds, lakes, and streams. Sometimes snails will be near the water's edge on marshy plants. In the Everglades, tree snails may be found on the trunks of trees above the water's surface.

SWALLOWTAIL BUTTERFLIES

Color: Tiger swallowtails are yellow with black stripes. Palamedes swallowtails are mostly blackish brown.
Size: Most swallowtails are 3–4 inches (7.6–10.2 cm) across. Tiger and palamedes swallowtails can be more than 5 inches (12.7 cm) across.
Food: Flower nectar.
Notes: Tiger swallowtails are common near streams or muddy, shallow ponds. Look for palamedes swallowtails in southern swamps around pickerel weed. The swallowtail is the state butterfly of Alabama, Arizona, Delaware, Oklahoma, South Carolina, and Tennessee, and the state insect of Oregon and Virginia.

CRAYFISH

Color: Brown.
Size: 3–5 inches (7.6–12.7 cm) long.
Food: Plants and small aquatic animals, even dead ones!
Notes: They usually hide during the day, but crayfish may be seen in the water on the bottom at the shallow edges of marshes, ponds, or streams. The crayfish is the state crustacean of Louisiana.

WATER STRIDER

Color: Dark brown or blackish.
Size: About $1/2$ inch (1.3 cm) long.
Food: Small insects.
Notes: Water striders look like they're skating across the quiet water of wetlands. Their feet have special hairs that help them float.

FISHING SPIDER

Color: Dark-brown body with white stripes, light-brown legs.
Size: Body $1/2$–$3/4$ inch (1.3–2.0 cm) long. Including legs, up to $2 1/2$ inches (6.4 cm) across.
Food: Small insects.
Notes: Look for these spiders walking over plants in swamps, marshes, ponds, or slow-moving streams east of the Rocky Mountains.

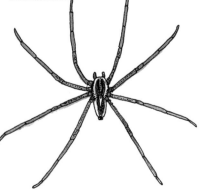

Mammals and Fish

RIVER OTTER
Color: Dark brown.
Size: 3–4 feet (1.0–1.3 m) long.
Food: Small fish and other small animals.
Notes: Look for river otters along riverbanks, both in and out of the water.

MOOSE
Color: Dark brown.
Size: About 6 ½–7 ½ feet (2.0–2.3 m) tall.
Food: Shrubs and other plants—often those found in or near water.
Notes: Moose are the largest of the deer family. Look for them standing in shallow lakes and ponds eating the plants growing there. The moose is the state land mammal of Alaska and the state animal of Maine.

MUSKRAT
Color: Brown.
Size: Body up to 2 feet (0.6 m) long.
Food: Mostly cattails and other aquatic plants.
Notes: Muskrat homes are burrows in stream banks or mounds of wetland plants that look like small beaver lodges.

MINK
Color: Brown, sometimes grayish.
Size: 19–28 inches (48–71 cm) long.
Food: Muskrats and other small- to medium-size animals.
Notes: Mink may live in an empty muskrat or beaver home or in hollow logs. They sometime dig stream-bank burrows. Look for the mink at night in marshes and along lakes, ponds, rivers, and creeks.

LARGEMOUTH BASS
Color: Silvery color with olive green on top and a dark band on each side.
Size: Typically 7–15 inches (17.8–38.1 cm), but can reach 27 inches (69 cm) long.
Food: Fish, frogs, crayfish, and aquatic insects.
Notes: Swims near the surface to eat small fish. Look in lakes, ponds, and streams where plants are growing out of the water. The largemouth bass is the state fish of Alabama, Florida, Georgia, Mississippi, and Tennessee.

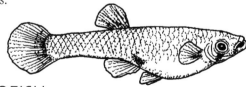

MOSQUITOFISH
Color: Silvery gray, darker on top.
Size: 1 ½–2 inches (3.8–5.1 cm) long.
Food: Small aquatic insects and frog eggs.
Notes: Look for these small fish in clear, shallow water, swimming around the plants near the shore. You may also see them at the water's surface.

Reptiles and Amphibians

BULLFROG

Color: Greenish yellow with blotches of dark gray or brown.

Size: Up to 8 inches (20.3 cm) long.

Food: Insects, crayfish, frogs, and small fish.

Notes: This is the largest frog in North America. It is most commonly found at night along the water's edge. The bullfrog is the state amphibian of Oklahoma.

CHORUS FROG

Color: Gray, brown, olive green, or green with darker stripes or spots on back.

Size: Usually less than 2 inches (5.1 cm) long.

Food: Insects.

Notes: The voice of chorus frogs sounds like "prreep, prreep" or like the sound of a fingernail dragged over the teeth of a small comb. Listen for them mostly at night as the weather warms up in the spring. Found in grassy wetland areas and some swamps.

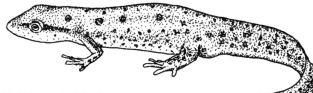

EASTERN NEWT

Color: Dark orange, olive green, light or dark brown.

Size: 1½–5½ inches (3.8–14.0 cm) long.

Food: Small aquatic animals.

Notes: Found in or near quiet water, usually in places with lots of submerged plants. Look for them in shallow water hunting for food.

POND SLIDER

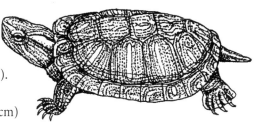

Color: Dark olive green or black with red edges on the carapace (the turtle's top shell). The head has yellow stripes.

Size: 4–10 inches (10.2–25.4 cm) long.

Food: Mostly plants but will also eat small animals.

Notes: Commonly seen sitting in the sun on logs or rocks. Look for them along lake edges and in streams, rivers, and other shallow, quiet water. Found in more areas of North America than any other turtle. The painted turtle is the state reptile of Michigan.

LEOPARD FROG

Color: Green, brownish, or gray, usually with dark spots.

Size: 2–5 inches (5–12.5 cm) long.

Food: Insects.

Notes: Look for these frogs at night in or near ponds, marshes, and other permanent water. They are also found among the plants at the water's edge and in wet meadows. The leopard frog is the state amphibian of Vermont.

RIBBON SNAKE

Color: Dark body with three light stripes, one on top and one on each side of the snake's body.

Size: Up to 4 feet (1.3 m) long.

Food: Frogs, tadpoles, salamanders, and small fish.

Notes: These snakes can swim quickly across the water's surface. Look for them among plants at the edges of lakes, ponds, marshes, and swamps, and in bogs.

Wildflowers and Carnivorous Plants

WATER LILY

Color: White flowers and green leaves.
Size: Leaves are 3–15 inches (7.5–37.5 cm) long.
Flowers are 3–5 inches (7.5–13 cm) wide.
Notes: Look on the quiet water of swamps, marshes, and ponds for leaves that float flat on the water's surface. Spatterdock, a type of yellow pond lily, has leaves that may not lie flat but stick up out of the water.

PURPLE LOOSESTRIFE

Color: Purplish pink flowers and green leaves.
Size: 2–4 feet (0.6–1.2 m) tall.
Notes: The purple loosestrife is found along roads, wet meadows, and many other places with water-soaked ground and is an introduced (non-native) plant.

ARROWHEAD

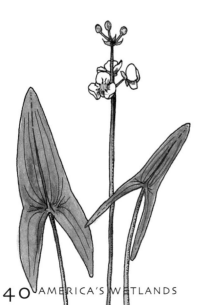

Color: White flowers and bright-green leaves.
Size: 1–4 feet (0.3–1.2 m) tall.
Notes: Look for this plant growing out of quiet water in all wetland regions of North America. Also called "wapato" and, more commonly, "duck potato," because waterfowl eat the plant's small, potatolike, underground stems.

SUNDEW

Color: Green leaves with reddish hairs and white or pinkish flowers.
Size: 4–9 inches (10.2–22.9 cm) tall.
Notes: Look for the carnivorous sundew in bogs. Sticky drops on the leaves attract and trap insects, which the plant eats.

PITCHER PLANTS

Color: Usually green with reddish purple or reddish brown flowers and veins. Some are yellow or yellowish green.
Size: 8–36 inches (20.3–91.4 cm) tall.
Notes: Most pitcher plants grow in bogs in eastern North America. The leaves form water-filled tubes lined with hairs that point downward. When insects enter the tube from the top they cannot get back out past the hairs, so they eventually drown in the water at the base of the tube. After they rot, this carnivorous plant absorbs them as food. The pitcher plant is the provincial flower of Newfoundland.

Shrubs

LABRADOR TEA

Color: White flower clusters and green leaves that turn brown as they get old.

Size: 1–4 feet (0.3–1.2 m) high.

Notes: Look for this plant in bogs and in places with peat. It is most common in Northeast and North wetlands with cold, wet ground.

BOG ROSEMARY

Color: Light-pink flowers and skinny leaves that are dark green on top and whitish underneath.

Size: Low shrub up to 18 inches (50 cm) high.

Notes: Bog rosemary is found with leatherleaf and Labrador tea in bogs. Look for the flowers in late spring.

WILLOW

Color: Green leaves. Green, reddish, or brown twigs; gray, brown, or black branches and trunk.

Size: Most willows are large shrubs up to 20 feet (6.1 m) tall.

Notes: Willows are very common, especially along shores of rivers and streams. There are many different kinds, often with narrow, pointed leaves. Birds sometimes use the fuzz from willow seeds in their nests.

RED-OSIER DOGWOOD

Color: White flowers, dark-red stems, and green leaves.

Size: 3–10 feet (0.9–3.0 m) tall.

Notes: This shrub or small tree grows along streams and rivers.

LEATHERLEAF

Color: White bell-shaped flowers and olive green leaves.

Size: 1–4 feet (0.3–1.2 m) high.

Notes: Look for this shrub in bogs and along the edges of lakes and ponds, sometimes growing out onto the surface of the water.

Ferns and Grasslike Plants

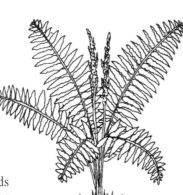

CINNAMON FERN

Color: Bright-green fronds (fern leaves) with brownish hairs at their base. In the spring, cinnamon-colored fronds grow in the center of the plant.
Size: 3–5 feet (0.9–1.5 m) tall.
Notes: This fern grows in swamps as a large, tall bunch of fronds. Cinnamon ferns are most common in eastern North America.

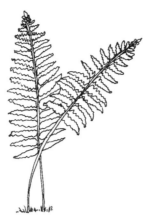

MARSH FERN

Color: Green fronds (fern leaves).
Size: Up to about 2½ feet (0.8 m) tall.
Notes: A very common fern especially in wet meadows of the eastern half of North America.

BULRUSH

Color: Light green to olive green stem, brownish flowers.
Size: 3–6½ feet (1–2 m) tall.
Notes: The bulrush grows in water along the edges of ponds and shallow lakes. Two common bulrushes are the hard-stem bulrush (also called tule) and the soft-stem bulrush. Both are soft and spongy inside the stem. Look for red-winged blackbirds sitting near the tops of the stems.

HORSETAIL

Color: Green.
Size: Up to about 3 feet (1 m) tall.
Notes: This plant has no true leaves, only leaflike "teeth" at joints on the stem. Horsetail is also called scouring rush because the stem can be pulled apart and each rough-sided, tubelike piece can be used to scour, or clean, dishes or pans. Look for them in swamps, marshes, and along the edges of streams.

SOFT RUSH

Color: Green stems with brownish green flowers.
Size: Up to 4 feet (1.2 m) tall.
Notes: Soft rush is found in marshes and swamps. Some wetland birds hide among the stems and muskrats eat the roots.

WILD RICE

Color: Green, turning brown by fall.
Size: 3–10 feet (0.9–3.0 m) tall.
Notes: Look for this tall grass in flooded areas and marshes. Also found along edges of ponds, lakes, and slow rivers, especially in the eastern half of North America. Wild rice is the state grain of Minnesota.

Trees

COTTONWOOD

Color: Bright-green leaves that turn yellow in fall; gray trunk.

Size: About 100 feet (30.5 m) tall.

Notes: Cottonwoods are common trees along the edges of rivers and streams. The name actually comes from the cottony seeds, not from the tree's wood. This is the state tree of Kansas, Nebraska, and Wyoming.

BALD CYPRESS

Color: Yellow-green, needlelike leaves. Bark is gray to reddish brown.

Size: Large trees up to 125 feet (38.1 m) tall.

Notes: Look around the base of the swollen trunk for pointed, wooden, stumplike things sticking out of the water or wet ground. These are part of the tree and are called "cypress knees." Botanists (scientists who study plants) aren't sure why the cypress knees grow this way, but some people think they provide air to the roots or perhaps they help support the tree in the wet soil. Bald cypress trees are very common in the swamps of the Southeast and sometimes have Spanish moss hanging from the branches. Bald cypress is the state tree of Louisiana.

OAK

Color: Green leaves and gray bark.

Size: The average oak is 50–80 feet (15.2–24.4 m) tall, but some types of oaks may grow to 100 feet (30.5 m) tall.

Notes: Look for oak trees in wet areas along streams, rivers, and swamps. Wood ducks eat acorns from oak trees. The live oak is the state tree of Georgia.

SYCAMORE

Color: Bark is dark brown on the surface and may peel off, exposing light-brown or whitish bark underneath. Leaves are large and green; the bottom of the leaf is lighter in color and often hairy.

Size: 60–100 feet (18.3–30.5 m) tall.

Notes: Sycamores grow along the shores of lakes, rivers, and swamps. Look for small brown balls hanging from the trees in the fall. These are clusters of dry fruits, each with a seed inside. In California, hummingbirds use the hairs from the large sycamore leaves to line their nests.

RED MAPLE and SILVER MAPLE

Color: Red maple has green leaves that turn red in the fall. Silver maple has green leaves that are silvery on the bottom side and turn light yellow in the fall. Both have light-gray bark.

Size: Up to 80 feet (24.4 m) tall.

Notes: Look for both trees in swamps and other areas with wet ground in the Southeast and Northeast regions. Sometimes they are both called swamp maple trees, and the silver maple may also be called a water maple. The red maple is the state tree of Rhode Island.

Animal Tracks and Signs

You can usually find some animals in wetland areas almost any time, but many may be hard to see clearly among the wetland plants or may be hiding. When that happens, check the ground for animal footprints, or tracks. Look in areas with mud, silt, or sand such as at the edges of streams and rivers and along the marshy edges of lakes and ponds. You might find tracks of ducks, geese, herons, and muskrats. You may also see tracks of raccoons or other animals that don't live in the water but go there to drink or find food. Trails and roads through wetland areas are also good places to look for animal tracks.

In addition to tracks, search for other animal signs. This might include the gnawed and pointed tree trunk cut by a beaver or piles of scat (animal poop) left by a moose or deer.

Identifying animal tracks and signs is fun and a good way to discover more about what types of animals live in the wetlands.

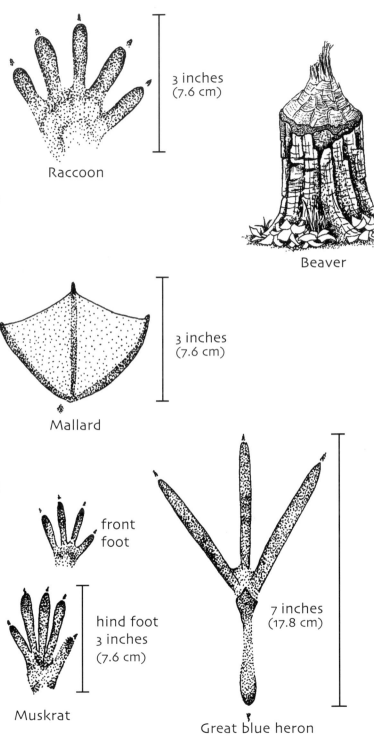

Raccoon

3 inches
(7.6 cm)

Beaver

Mallard

3 inches
(7.6 cm)

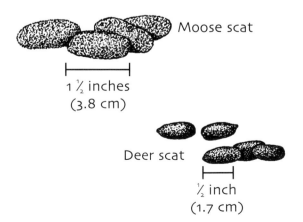

Moose scat

1 ½ inches
(3.8 cm)

Deer scat

½ inch
(1.7 cm)

front foot

hind foot
3 inches
(7.6 cm)

Muskrat

7 inches
(17.8 cm)

Great blue heron

Glossary

Aquatic: A plant or animal that lives in water or needs water for part of its life cycle.

Bayou: The name for a slow-moving stream or river, especially in Louisiana and Mississippi.

Bog: An old lake or pond with plants such as sphagnum moss growing across the surface, above floating layers of peat. Gets all of its water from rain. Bog water is acidic with low amounts of oxygen so very few plants can survive in a bog.

Creek: A small stream.

Drought: A period with no rain that can last for many months or even a year or more.

Fen: Similar to a bog but less acidic and with more oxygen and nutrients for plants to grow. Water in a fen comes from groundwater and water runoff.

Lake: A large area of water surrounded by land. Streams or rivers flow into and out of lakes.

Marsh: An area with soggy ground that is flooded at least part of the year. Grasses and other herblike plants are the most common plants. Trees are not usually found in marshes.

Migratory (Migration): Something that moves from one place to another. Often refers to animals that spend summers in cooler, northern areas and winters in warmer regions to the south.

Mudflat: The shallow, muddy area along the edges of lakes and rivers that becomes exposed when the water level goes down.

Muskeg: A type of swamp formed from a bog and containing black spruce trees and sphagnum moss. Found in the northern part of North America.

Peat: Dead plant material that has piled up underwater over a long time and is rotting very, very slowly. A "peatland" is a wetland area where peat moss, or sphagnum moss, has built up over many years.

Pond: A small body of water surrounded by land.

Pothole: A type of pond or shallow lake in the northern part of the Midwest. They were created from melted chunks of ice left behind by glaciers during the last ice age.

River: A large stream of flowing water that eventually empties into a lake or the ocean.

Slough: A slow-moving creek in a marsh, ditch, or other low spot.

Stream: Like a river only much smaller.

Swamp: A place with trees or shrubs that is always wet or covered with at least a few inches of water except during drought.

Waterfowl: Birds that need to live on or near water such as ducks, geese, and swans.

Resources

The places listed below have wetland areas open to the public. They may also have hiking trails, a visitor center, and a naturalist or ranger to answer questions. Write to them for more information or search for them on the Internet.

SOUTHEAST

Big Thicket National Preserve
3785 Milam
Beaumont, TX 77701

Everglades National Park
40001 State Road 9336
Homestead, FL 33034

Great Dismal Swamp National Wildlife Refuge
3100 Desert Road
Suffolk, VA 23434

Okefenokee National Wildlife Refuge
Route 2, Box 3330
Folkston, GA 31537

NORTHEAST

Acadia National Park
P.O. Box 177
Eagle Lake Road
Bar Harbor, ME 04609-0177

Great Swamp National Wildlife Refuge
152 Pleasant Plains Road
Basking Ridge, NJ 07920

Horicon National Wildlife Refuge
W4279 Headquarters Road
Mayville, WI 53050

MIDWEST

Cheyenne Bottoms Wildlife Area
56 NE 40 Road
Great Bend, KS 67530

Long Lake National Wildlife Refuge
12000 353rd Street SE
Moffit, ND 58560-9704

WEST

Bear River Migratory Bird Refuge
58 South 950 West
Brigham City, UT 84302

Deer Flat National Wildlife Refuge
13751 Upper Embankment Road
Nampa, ID 83686

PACIFIC

Nisqually National Wildlife Refuge
100 Brown Farm Road
Olympia, WA 98516-2399

NORTH

Arctic National Wildlife Refuge
101 12th Avenue Room 236
Box 20
Fairbanks, AK 99701

Wapusk National Park
P.O. Box 127
Churchill, Manitoba
R0B 0E0 Canada

Common and Scientific Names

Before a trip into the swamps of the Southeast, some people may tell you to watch out for a poisonous snake called the cottonmouth. Other people may warn you about the poisonous water moccasin. They are actually different names for the same snake. Common names for plants and animals may be different depending upon who you talk to or what you're using to look up information. It can be very confusing. But the **scientific name** of a plant or animal is always the same everywhere in the world.

Scientific names have two parts. The first part is called the *genus* and is capitalized. The second part is called the *species* and is not capitalized. Both parts are underlined or typed in *slanted* letters called italics. If the common name refers to more than one species of the same genus, then the species name is left out and "spp." is written instead.

This list includes all the plants and animals illustrated in this book.

Index

Cottonmouth or Water moccasin
(*Agkistrondon piscivorus*)